S0-EAW-742

The Journey

Kenneth Jernigan
Editor

Large Type Edition

A KERNEL BOOK
published by
NATIONAL FEDERATION OF THE BLIND

Cover Photograph: NASA/PHOTRI

Table of Contents

Kenneth Jernigan, President Emeritus
National Federation of the Blind

EDITOR'S INTRODUCTION

This is the second Kernel Book to be issued this year, and the fifth in the series. The first Kernel Book was published in 1991, just over two years ago.

When we started the series, we hoped it would reach a wide audience and bring a new understanding about blindness—that it would show blind people as they really are, ordinary human beings with the normal range of wants and wits, strengths and weaknesses. I think it is fair to say that we are well on the way to achieving that objective—or, at least, that we have made substantial progress toward it.

We have now published more than two million Kernel Books, and the demand for them shows no sign of diminishing. An increasing number of people (very often strangers I meet as I travel over the country) tell me they have read more than one of these books and now feel that a great deal of the mystery has gone out of blindness for them. These strangers (they usually don't stay strangers) feel comfortable in asking me questions about blindness—how a blind person travels from place to place, how clothes are selected, and how the ordinary tasks of daily living are performed. But they also feel comfortable talking about personal matters—how it feels to be blind, and everything from perception of color to courtship and marriage.

This, of course, is what we hoped would happen. The people whose stories appear in these pages are mostly just like you except that they can't see. This doesn't give them unusual talents, such as improved hearing or special musical ability; nor does it curse them with unbearable burdens. If those of us who are blind have appropriate training and equal opportunity, we can get along as well as anybody else—earning our own way, having a family, and leading a regular life. And, after all, isn't that really the way it is with you? If you didn't have a chance for an education and if everybody thought you were incompetent and inferior, isn't that pretty much the way it would be? That's how it is with the blind. In short, if we have a chance and good training, we'll do all right, neither needing nor wanting custody or care.

And one more thing: We want you to know about the National Federation of the Blind. Established in 1940, this organization has, in the opinion of most of us who know about such things, been the single most important factor in helping blind people stand on their own feet and do for themselves. We who are blind still have a long way to go, but we are getting there—and the Kernel Books are helping.

Some of you already know many of the people you will meet in this volume. Others will be new to you. Whether you are a first-time reader or have been with us from the beginning of the series, I hope you will find the present volume interesting and informative. If you have questions about blindness or know somebody who needs our help, let us know. Meanwhile, here is the fifth Kernel Book. It tells of a journey—a journey which, in its own way, is as significant as the trek across the prairie in the last century by the pioneers, or the landing on the moon in the present century. It is the journey of the blind from second-class status to hope and opportunity.

Kenneth Jernigan
Baltimore, Maryland
1993

WHY LARGE TYPE

The type size used in this book is 14 Point for two important reasons: One, because typesetting of 14 Point or larger complies with federal standards for the printing of materials for visually impaired readers, and we wanted to show you exactly what type size is necessary for people with limited sight.

The second reason is because many of our friends and supporters have asked us to print our paperback books in 14 Point type so they too can easily read them. Many people with limited sight do not use Braille. We hope that by printing this book in a larger type than customary, many more people will be able to benefit from it.

Kenneth Jernigan in front of the barn on his boyhood farm in Tennessee.

THE VALUE OF PLANNING

by Kenneth Jernigan

Blind children are as different from each other as sighted children, but this may not hold for every characteristic. If, for instance, blind children want to get along and do well, they have to learn to plan. At least I did.

As I have often said, living on a farm in rural Tennessee in the late twenties and early thirties was altogether different from what we know today. Not only did we not have a radio, a telephone, electricity, running water, indoor plumbing, or a newspaper. We didn't have automobiles either. It wasn't that we didn't know what a car was. It was just that one didn't pass our house on an average of more than once a week. When we wanted to go somewhere, we walked, rode a horse, or traveled in a wagon drawn by two mules.

Besides me, there were three others in that four-room house, my father and mother and a brother, who was four years older than I. Visitors were rare, and the other members of the family were usually busy. As to entertainment, it was scarce—and even reading wasn't available until after I went away to school in Nashville when I was six.

In the circumstances I had to make my shots count, both for the short run and the long run. Early on, I knew that an education was essential if I didn't want to spend the rest of my life in isolation on the farm, which I didn't. I also knew that there would be a fairly brief window of time to set things in motion.

After I started school, I spent nine months of every year in Nashville and three months at home on the farm. That meant that I pretty much lost contact with any local children who might have grown up as friends, and it also meant that I would have three months of isolation and boredom if I didn't find something productive to do. And I didn't just want entertainment. Well, that too—but something more, something that would help me get an education, something that would help me get off the farm.

By the time I was in the sixth grade I had started getting Braille and recorded books from the Library of Congress. I ordered from the main library in Washington, from a library in Cincinnati, and from another in Illinois. I don't know whether I was supposed to use only one, but I didn't think it was safe to ask, believing I had better let well enough alone. I spent my summers reading, sometimes (not always but sometimes) twenty hours a day—and I took notes on every book I read, planning to be able to make top grades when I got to college, with time left over for participation in extracurricular activities. I thought this would help me build a record of not just being a book worm. By the time I finished high school I had read hundreds of books and had stacks of bulging folders of Braille notes.

In my senior year of high school (that would have been 1945) I had my first con-

tact with the federal-state rehabilitation program. A counselor came to the School for
the Blind, and he and I sat down for a chat
in what was called "the parlor." (The school
was in an old southern mansion, and the
amenities lingered, high-ceilinged parlor and
all.) When we got past the niceties, the
counselor asked me what I wanted to major
in when I went to college. I told him I
wanted to be a lawyer. He left the subject,
talked for a while about the crops and the
weather, and then circled back to it. He
asked me to tell him three or four things I
might like to do.

I was a late teenager (maybe a brash
one), so I told him I didn't need to give him
three or four. I wanted to be a lawyer. He
was not an unkind man, but when you cut
through the verbiage, what he said was
clear. I could either be a lawyer and pay for
it myself, or I could be something else and
the rehabilitation agency would help. Aca-
demically I was prepared for college, and I
had done what I could as a blind boy grow-
ing up on a farm to save money. Also, my

dad and mother were willing to do what they could to help. But all of it together wasn't enough, in addition to which I didn't feel right about putting strains on the family finances. In short, I went to college and was something else.

As I have said, the rehabilitation counselor was not an unkind man, and he undoubtedly thought he was acting in my best interest; but I now know that he was wrong. There are, to my personal knowledge, hundreds of successfully practicing blind lawyers in this country today. If the National Federation of the Blind had been stronger at the time and if I had known of its existence, maybe things would have been different. Or, maybe they turned out all right after all.

In any case I started college in the fall of 1945, but the day before I was to enroll, I became seriously ill with a ruptured appendix. So I was six weeks late.

Tennessee Tech is located in the hills of upper middle Tennessee, and before the Second World War it had only four or five hundred students. Now, in the fall of 1945, it suddenly had a student body of 2,000, most of them combat hardened veterans. I was the only blind student on the campus, and even though my rigorous planning stood me in good stead, there were touchy moments.

When I went to my first English class, for instance, the teacher said to me publicly: "Young man, you there on the back row, I don't object to your being in my class, but I think it is only fair to tell you that you will fail. A blind person can't do college English." I said I hoped I would get a fair opportunity to try, and he assured me that I would.

Later, the biology teacher was blunter and more terse. I had decided to sit on the front row this time, and the teacher was neither gentle nor kindly disposed. He had obviously had a run-in with the college administration because of me, and he wasn't happy. His speech went to this effect:

"You can sit in this class if you want to, but I can tell you right now that you will fail. I didn't want you here, but the dean made me take you."

When I ventured to say that I hoped I would have an equal opportunity, he replied with what I can only call menace, "Don't worry! You will!"

The next day in laboratory I learned what he meant. There were four of us at each lab table, and I was handed a microscope along with the rest. When I asked what he wanted me to do with it, he said, "It's not my problem. You said you wanted an equal opportunity. Here's your microscope."

Let me not be misunderstood. Almost uniformly I was treated with understanding and respect, and even the English and biology teachers eventually came around. The first quarter each of them gave me a B, but after that I got A's. As a matter of fact, the biology teacher became as belligerently my defender as he had been my detractor.

As the college years went by, I made the grades I had hoped and planned to make, but an experience in my senior year is worth noting. I had become so accustomed to being able to make A's that perhaps I had become careless, or maybe just a little too big for my pants. I had all of the credits I needed to graduate, but just for fun I enrolled in a class for advanced athletes. I was reasonably good at standing on my hands and other gymnastics, but I was totally outclassed. When the coach told me he was going to have to give me a B, I was not disappointed but grateful. Inwardly I felt that I probably deserved an F for presumption. I had no business enrolling in the class in the first place. From that experience I learned a valuable lesson, one that has stood me in good stead for the rest of my life.

I not only made the good grades for which I had prepared during the summers of my boyhood on the farm, but I took part in intercollegiate debating, became a member of the editorial staff of the college newspaper, and got elected to a variety of club and class offices. In addition, I helped pay my college expenses by selling candy, tobacco products, and sundries.

When I finished my degree at Tennessee Tech, I went on to graduate school and later into teaching and other activities, but the basis of it all (the underpinning which made it possible) was the early preparation, the habit of planning I developed as a child.

Today's blind youngsters are, by and large, not discouraged from going to college, and Braille and recorded books are more plentiful than they have ever been. But there are still major obstacles to the blind person seeking a career and a full life. The National Federation of the Blind is now strong enough in every part of the land to play a major role, and public attitudes are better than they used to be. Even so, one thing is unchanged. Planning is still the essential foundation of success.

Barbara Walker: Mother and community leader.

THE SOLO

by Barbara Walker

For all of us, life is full of choices. A frequent choice those of us who are blind face is whether to accept more help than we really need (thus furthering misconceptions which exist about us) or to refuse such help and risk creating a scene or causing embarrassment to a valued colleague. Here Barbara Walker describes just such a situation.

It is often hard to know where to draw the line between acceptance of what is and the necessity to take a stand for change. And for me, mostly this struggle has been played out in little things. One such instance involved my singing a solo in church.

For quite some time, the choir director at my church had been asking me to sing a solo. She said people had approached her wanting me to do that, and wanting her to encourage me, since they knew I wouldn't be likely to request the privilege when opportunities were given to do so. I had finally agreed to invite my sister to come and sing a duet with me, but it became obvious that our church schedules were such that it might be a long time before that would be workable. The director's next request was that I choose something to sing and perhaps a member of the choir to sing with, and ask an accompanist for assistance in that area if I preferred not to play my guitar.

All of those seemed like "piece of cake" kinds of things to her, I'm sure. But for me, a person whose ministry through music is not an assertive one, those suggestions sounded unthinkable. Assuming I had the nerve to approach another choir member to sing with me (which I didn't), how would the person respond?

Also, I learn music by hearing it and memorizing it. I don't do solos, and don't have a storehouse of options to present to a potential accompanist. As I stood before the director in the presence of a friend with whom I ride to choir, I felt the familiar longing to be assertive struggling with the urge to run to some place where I could be inconspicuous.

The visible result of that struggle was a period of silence followed by an explanation to her of the situation as I saw it. I wanted so much to be able to thank her for her suggestions and follow them through. But the mere thought of doing that constricted my throat, weakened my knees, and sent my tongue between my teeth to stifle their chattering. Ultimately, I reminded her that I was not a soloist requesting an opportunity to perform, but a servant shyly preparing to answer a call to minister. The potential duet discussed that night also fell through due to scheduling difficulties.

Shortly after that, I received a call from the director asking if I would sing a short portion of an upcoming anthem as a solo. Knowing that although it was a familiar hymn tune the lyrics were different, I said I would be glad to do that, but would need someone to read the words to me before we practiced it. I said I would bring my Braille 'n Speak for that purpose.

During practice, when it came time to work on that anthem she announced that I would be singing the first verse. She had all of the women sing it through one time, and I entered the words into my Braille 'n Speak as they sang. There was one part I didn't understand, so I asked for clarification of it before singing it myself as she had requested. Her response both surprised and humiliated me. "Oh, just sing the words you know, or sing la la la. They'll love whatever you do, and no one will know if you're singing what's written or not.

There it was again—the old "anything you do will be wonderful, honey" routine. Suddenly the most surprising thing to me was why I still, after all these years, find it catching me off guard. I sat for a moment in the silence of belittlement, thinking thoughts of the obvious: "She would know. The choir would know. God would know." And as the silence seemed to be melting into the rustling of papers and shifting of weight on chairs, I heard my voice from somewhere saying, "I would know."

With the barely audible prompting of a fellow choir member who has often responded to my real requests for her assistance rather than her imaginings of what I might need, I rather feebly sang my renewed commitment to love and serve Jesus. Before leaving that night, the director, the accompanist and I agreed to meet in the sanctuary on Sunday morning prior to the service to practice with the microphone.

When I arrived in the sanctuary on Sunday, the director was talking to the sound control person. She announced to me that he would place a microphone on a stand and someone would assist me to it and stand by me while I sang. I felt again the grip of incredulity. For years, I had been processing and recessing with the choir, not to mention coming in and out of the choir loft and chancel area for various other purposes.

Struggling to keep my composure, I found myself asking the kind, bubbly, victim of society's insistence that I be cared for—this choir director whose spirit and freedom to be uninhibited I receive as gifts to cherish—questions which sounded harsh and unrelenting.

"Do you think of me as an adult? Why is it necessary that I use the microphone differently from how others have used it? What is it that causes people to cast reality and experience to the wind and insist that everything be different when working with a blind person?" At once, her breezy confidence turned into wind-swept confusion. We were swirling toward a trap of absurdity—she wanting to protect me, I wanting to educate her, both wanting to serve Jesus.

As each of us shared our concern with the other, we came to terms with the situation. Since only the women were singing that day, I agreed to sit in the front rather than in my usual place in the second row. The standing microphone would be in front of me. Pride wanted me to insist that I sit in my usual row and walk down to the microphone. Knowledge said others who prefer not to be conspicuous have sat by the microphone or had it passed to them where they're seated. Reason suggested I accept the plan. Wisdom concurred, reminding me I was there to minister, not to win a contest of wills.

At home after the service, I discussed the situation with my children. They were both glad I hadn't allowed the original scenario to prevail. John, my eight-year-old, said it wouldn't have been right. Marsha, my ten-year-old, elaborated. "I would have been embarrassed," she said, "not because anyone should be ashamed to get help if it's needed, but because you wouldn't need that help and you and we would know it." She felt that for me to accept that option would be to deny progress.

I recalled the fierce independence of their deceased father, who had treated his blindness as a characteristic which, although causing some inconvenience, would not have its existence used as a basis for buying into society's notion that it should debilitate him. I also thought of the tens of thousands of us in the National Federation of the Blind who daily deal with struggles such as this one. I hoped we had all taken a small step forward.

Since that day, I have sung two additional short solos. One was at a Sunday evening service, at which I walked to the microphone from a place in the congregation and returned to my seat during the remainder of the song. The other occasion was during a regular service, and the choir director previously mentioned was again in charge. This time, I stayed in my usual place and was handed the mike just prior to my solo. There was no discussion, no confusion, no trouble at all.

The message I sang that day was: "God of many names, gathered into one, in your glory come and meet us, moving, endlessly becoming." And as it happened within me and within the Trinity Church choir director, it happened for all of us. We are all "moving, endlessly becoming," and that is a marvelous source of hope.

Kathy Kannenberg with her math
class at Ligon Middle School.

SHE MAKES THINGS FUNNER

by Colin Soloway

Often news articles about blindness focus on the old stereotypes of hopelessness and helplessness. However, with increasing frequency, refreshingly enlightened reporters are beginning to tell the real story of blindness. Here Colin Soloway, writing for the Raleigh, North Carolina News & Observer, *details the experiences of Kathy Kannenberg during her first year as an elementary school math teacher.*

Kathy Kannenberg always loved school, but when she was in fourth grade, her teacher considered her a discipline problem.

"She asked me to read what was on the board, and I told her there wasn't anything on the board. She asked me again, and I told her again," Kathy said. "She thought I was smart-mouthing her, and she made me stay after class to write 'I WILL NOT MOCK THE TEACHER' 100 times on the board."

But Kathy still insisted that there was nothing on the board. When she went to see the principal with her parents, a quick eye exam by the school nurse found that Kathy wasn't a troublemaker: She was legally blind.

Kathy's experience didn't sour her on school. She stayed in the classroom for the next 15 years, as a student, and finally as a teacher.

Now, in her first year at Ligon Middle School, Kathy teaches her sixth-graders more than math and science. Every day, she shows them that physical disability need not limit their ambitions or their achievements. Her efforts quickly have won her the admiration of her students, their parents and other teachers.

At midday, Kathy, tall and slender, patrols the aisles of her math class as her students arrange counting chips on their desks. Trying to give them a hands-on understanding of algebraic equations with single variables, she moves from student to student, probing to see if each student grasps the concepts the game pieces represent.

She calls each child by name. She steps confidentially between the desks. An observer never would suspect she is blind.

Kathy, 23, says that despite her deteriorating vision, caused by rheumatoid arthritis, there is nothing she would rather be doing than standing in front of a class.

"I love teaching," she said. "I always seem to be in that role."

The principal who employed Kathy said her blindness was not a consideration "either way" in her being hired.

"She was hired absolutely on her ability," he said. "We were just tickled pink to find someone to teach both math and science. But I think Kathy's disability and the way she deals with it bring something special to the classroom."

Outside the classroom, Kathy devotes herself to a broader goal: to educate the public about the circumstances and problems of the blind and visually impaired, and assist people with disabilities in leading productive lives.

Recently elected president of the North Carolina chapter of the National Federation of the Blind, Kathy works for the rights of the visually impaired. In the forthcoming session of the General Assembly, she hopes to see a bill passed requiring that blind children, or children threatened with eventual blindness, be exposed to Braille at the same time sighted children are taught to read.

Kathy seems to pursue challenges wherever they present themselves. When she was younger, she went to work at a local stable in exchange for riding lessons. She still rides whenever she can. She said her students were shocked to see a photograph of her on horseback.

"They asked me if that was really me," she said. "Then they asked if there was someone with a rope leading the horse. I told them it was just me."

When Kathy walks outside of class, she carries a white cane, but in the classroom, she finds her ways by different cues.

"At first the children wanted to find out how far they could get away with spitballs, but sight isn't the only way to figure out who's doing what."

Kathy's principal said he has been impressed with her teaching this fall:

"I think she has been wonderful with both the children and their parents. The kids love her, and she won parents over immediately when she talked about handicaps to them at orientation."

Kathy described her first encounter with her students' parents at the open house before school started.

"I stood up in front of them, and I told them, 'I guarantee you that at least one person here is handicapped. Can you guess who it is?' They looked around at each other, and then I told them it was me."

Kathy says her discussion with the parents made them more comfortable with her.

"I've got a couple of students in the class who are learning disabled, and I think their parents understand that I understand what it is like to be at a disadvantage."

When asked to talk about their teacher, students in Kathy's sixth-grade learning skills class didn't mention her eyesight, or lack thereof. Instead they talked about what a good teacher she is, how much they like her and how much they feel she cares about them and what they are learning.

"She always says there are no dumb questions," one student said. "If you get something wrong, she'll make sure you understand it."

Another student said, "She explains, and keeps on explaining until we get it."

"She makes things a lot funner," said a student named Robert. "She makes sure everybody understands what she's talking about. On a scale of 1 to 10, I would give her an 11." His classmates shouted their approval.

Gary Wunder and daughter Missy

WHO IS RESPONSIBLE FOR WHOM?

by Gary Wunder

Gary Wunder is an articulate man of greater than average sensitivity and insight into the human condition. He is also a father and husband; a member of the National Federation of the Blind National Board; and president of the NFB of Missouri. He has been blind since birth. Here Gary relates an incident which occurred when he was out walking with his daughter.

I am the blind parent of a sighted child. My daughter was four years old when we were out walking one day. Now, there have been times when my daughter knew that I knew everything and times when my daughter was sure I knew nothing. We were going through one of those "I don't think he knows very much" stages. Whether that happened because of something that somebody at preschool said to her about having a blind father, or because it just happens in the development of children, I don't know. So, we were out walking one day. I've always walked with a cane, and I've always taken care of Missy—never had one accident whatsoever. But when we came up to the curb, she said, "Stop, Daddy, stop!"

I was surprised, and I said "Missy, I know to stop."

"How do you know?" said Missy.

"My cane falls off the curb," I said.

"Oh, Yeah. Well, don't go Daddy, don't go."

"Missy, I'm not going to go."

"Well, you can't see the light!"

"No, I can't see the light, but I can tell when to go by the traffic. Do you know what I mean?"

"Huh, uh."

"Well, when the traffic parallel to me is going, it's safe to go. When the traffic perpendicular is going, it's not safe. Do you know what I mean?"

"No, what's perpendicular?"

So I explained to her that parallel is that traffic moving on my right and perpendicular are those cars sitting out here in front of me. We waited a while, and Missy says, "Go, Daddy, go." I said, "Missy, the traffic in front of me is still going. It's not safe."

She said, "I know. I just wanted to see did you know."

So we cross the street when the light (and the traffic) changes. And no sooner do we get across than this woman bends down and gives my daughter a hug, and she said "Oh, you do such a good job with him."

It is at times like this I realize that, although we have come a long way in changing public understanding about blindness, we still have quite a distance to go. It was easier for the stranger on the corner to believe that my four year-old daughter possessed the maturity and understanding to deal with traffic and intersections than it was for her to believe that I, as a blind person, could be responsible for my own safety—let alone that of my daughter. It is at times like this also, that I renew my commitment to work as hard as I can in the National Federation of the Blind.

WHAT'S A SPITBALL?

by Barbara Pierce

Every year the National Federation of the Blind conducts a seminar for the parents of blind children at its National Convention. Often parents attending the seminar have never met successful blind adults and have not had the chance to talk with other parents of blind children. It is a time for offering encouragement and advice, a time for sharing hopes and fears. Barbara Pierce has been blind since childhood and is the mother of three children, who are now adults. Here is what she had to say to parents of blind children at our recent parents' seminar.

My last child just graduated from high school, which means that, for better or worse, I've done what I can as a parent—except for paying the college bills and worrying. I'm in effect finished with what I can do to shape my children, which in turn means that I will necessarily begin to forget all the tough times. This makes me an expert, but I hope you will take what I have to say seriously, despite my now lofty status.

One of the most important jobs that parents have to do is to set standards and to communicate those standards to their children. We do that all the time. Probably the most frequently used and least effective method we employ as parents is nagging: "Tuck in your shirt." "Keep your mouth closed when you chew." "Have you written that thank-you note?": those kinds of things.

Far more pervasively and more effectively, we establish standards in our children's lives by example and by expectation. This is certainly true in every area of life, but it is nowhere more evident than in teaching blindness-connected skills and attitudes. For after all, your blind children, whether they be your students or your own youngsters, are surrounded by some pretty lousy attitudes and some pretty low standards.

Your job is to wave the flag and to make sure that the expectations and the standards they adopt as their own are high. What your attitudes are will, in significant measure, determine what your children think about blindness and think about themselves as blind people. So you've got to be careful and watchful and mindful at all times about what it is that you are doing and saying and demonstrating and communicating to your child.

You should keep a close eye on what sighted children of your youngster's own age and ability level are doing. Are they choosing their own clothing in the morning? Then your child ought to be learning that stripes and plaids—whatever those are— don't go together, that red and orange are not a happy combination, that Bermuda shorts are not the appropriate thing to wear to church on Sunday morning. Blind children need to learn those things, and they don't learn them by having the clothes plunked down on the bottom of their beds every morning for them with the instruction to climb into them.

Do you expect your other children to do chores around the house? Then don't give the blind child the easy ones. The way to make siblings dislike a blind child is always to give him or her the easy things to do or always to let the blind kid off:

"But it's hard. I didn't get the window clean because I can't see it."

"Go back and do it again, kid." As a parent or a teacher, you've got to keep your standards high.

I remember being twelve. My mother didn't know other blind children. It was I who discovered that my friends all washed their own hair. At that time we set our hair and slept on curlers. Remember? They were all doing that for themselves. I wasn't, and I brought this to my mother's attention.

I hope that, as alert parents, you would be the ones to notice this and bring it to your child's attention. She simply didn't have any way of recognizing that gap, but she had the wit and the good sense to say, "Here's the shampoo. I think it'll be easier for you the first time to go wash it in the basement than in the bathtub. Shout when you think it's clean, and I'll check you." That was the last time she had anything to do with washing my hair. You've got to be alert to that sort of situation.

When a blind or low vision person drops something and doesn't see where it lands, it is appropriate for that person, in an orderly, efficient way, to search the area. It is no more inappropriate to search with the hands in an orderly fashion for something than it is to glance around and survey an area to see where the thing landed and pick it up. You do not benefit the child by always handing back things that have been dropped. A child will not be discouraged from dropping a stylus on the floor constantly if you always retrieve it.

Worry when your child comes home in the fifth grade and says, "Teacher says I don't have to take spelling tests." Since when was it okay for your child to have fewer grades in spelling than everybody else? The message given is that spelling is not important for a blind child. Object.

Worry when your high school sophomore dreads for an entire semester the assignment of the research paper and then comes home higher than a kite because she's just been told by her English teacher that he realizes research would be extremely hard for her, and therefore if she will do a little bit of research and then sit down and tell him about it on a cassette tape, that will be sufficient. That child has just lost seventy-five percent of the value of a research paper.

As an old English teacher and as the wife of an English professor, I can tell you that the discipline of organizing your thinking, shaping it into paragraphs, finding the right words, spelling them accurately, punctuating them correctly, and then figuring out a way of getting them legibly presented for consideration by the teacher is a significant measure of the discipline. Since when did your child not need that kind of practice in order to succeed in life?

Be careful when you see your child trying to use blindness as an excuse for getting out of punishment. Now it's confession time. I hadn't thought about this story in years. I was in the seventh grade when somebody in my home room sent a spitball toward the homeroom teacher, and he didn't know who the offender was. The guy didn't stand up and confess. Nobody would rat on him, so the teacher said, "All right, you all stay in for detention until somebody tells me who did this." Whenever I missed my school bus, I had to take the streetcar unless I worked it out with my mother that she'd pick me up from school. I wasn't certain of the route home on that streetcar. I was nervous about it. I didn't want to have to stay after school for detention. It wasn't convenient or helpful to me.

I walked up to that man and said, "I don't think that I was guilty of doing whatever it was, but would you tell me what a spitball is?" The man should have known that any twelve-year-old knows what a spitball is, even if she's not certain about how to propel it through the air at the speed with which that one had come at him.

He should have said to me, "You'll stay a week longer than everybody else does," but he didn't. His eyes misted over, and he told me that I certainly didn't have to stay. I am ashamed to admit this to you.

Here is another one. Your youngster brings to you the English assignment that has just been laboriously typed on the typewriter, and you discover that the two-year-old was messing with the keyboard and flipped the stencil key or that the typewriter ribbon ran out. What do you do then? You don't say, "I'll write a note tomorrow telling the teacher that you really did it, but that, because you are blind, you didn't notice that the print wasn't on the page."

Independence is going where you want to, when you want to, and doing what you want to by yourself, organizing what you want to do and getting it done. If you can do that, whether you're using readers or taxis or canes or a dog, you're independent. It is important that you understand that that's what constitutes independence.

Your job is to teach your child and the people around your child the value of some of the things that are so very important about blindness: why it is necessary for a blind youngster to master Braille and to be able to use a slate and stylus efficiently, rapidly, and effectively and why it's important for your child to be doing all of the schoolwork.

How do you know what the most important things are? You look around you. You find blind adults who are the kind of people you would like to see your child grow up to be. And you can be sure that if that person is the kind of person that you hope your child will be, then the standards and the attitudes that person has are probably the ones you want to instill in your youngster. You read the National Federation of the Blind's *Braille Monitor* and *Future Reflections* (its magazine for the parents of blind children). You read the articles and ponder them in your heart.

Your child will grow and begin to have the solid, strong attitudes about blindness that will result in his or her living a full and productive life, and your job will be complete.

WHERE AM I?

by Peggy Pinder

Peggy Pinder is no stranger to readers of previous Kernel Books. Here she tells of experiences she had as a teenager—experiences which laid the foundation for her career as a successful blind lawyer.

I am a lawyer, living in Iowa with a Yale Law School degree, five years of prosecutorial experience behind me, and a private practice. I am also blind.

In the course of my practice, I have appeared in courts in states other than my own. When this is done, the out-of-town lawyer needs to have a local lawyer to help with local procedures. I was representing a blind woman several years ago in a case in a different state. As we had worked things out between us, I was serving as "lead counsel," and he was "second chair." As the terms imply, the lead counsel sits in the first chair nearest to the judge.

When we walked into the courtroom, I happened to be in front of Allan, the local person when we reached the bar. I walked through the gate first, around the table to the plaintiff's side, and up to the first chair. Allan followed and stood behind the second chair. I could tell he was bemused by something as he made the introductions, but I didn't learn until later just what had happened.

As I came around the table and stopped behind the first chair, the judge nearly fell off the bench, motioning to Allan to enforce usual courtroom procedure. It never occurred to the judge that I might be a lawyer. He knew the plaintiff was a blind woman, and he thought that I was the plaintiff. He thought I did not know where I was or where I was going and that I was inadvertently breaking courtroom etiquette which dictates that the plaintiff sit in the seat farthest from the judge. He hoped to remedy the situation by silent hand and facial motions between himself and my "lawyer" so that court could proceed with everyone in their proper places.

Without ever indicating to the judge that he understood the signals, Allan as a good local lawyer quickly and efficiently made introductions, identifying me as lead counsel. He also mentioned that the plaintiff (as is permissible) was not there for argument on the motion. The judge subsided.

I just wish the judge had spoken directly to me and straightened out the misunderstanding with me instead of attempting to do it silently and without my knowledge. I think I would have felt better about it if he had. But, I also would have understood very well how he reached the conclusion that I did not know where I was. I thought the same thing for years.

When I first lost my sight, I was suddenly the only blind person I knew. There were no role models of successful, capable blind persons in my life. I only knew what I thought blind people could do: not much. I thought that college would be impossible for me now, that a job was out of the question, that these considerations were far too abstract to worry about because I now had a much bigger problem on my hands: How would I know where I was if I was blind?

I had always known where I was with visual cues—street signs, the appearance of buildings, store names above the doors, tables and chair in a room. Now, as a blind person, none of this was available to me. How would I know where I was? The best way to handle this problem was never to go anywhere. So, I mostly didn't.

My family urged me to get out and do things like everybody else. I did every now and then, just to please them. But, I didn't like it, and I did as little as I could. I didn't have any skills in getting information as a blind person, and I didn't have any way of finding any. I didn't know any other blind people who did get around on their own. I figured it couldn't be done.

And, when my family insisted that a blind person can do things, I would say to myself: "Yeah, sure. That's easy for you to say. But, you don't have to do it and feel stupid and clumsy and not know where you are. You have your sight. That makes all the difference." I knew they meant well, but they couldn't teach me the skills. They didn't know them, and they didn't use them.

All this occurred during high school, a hard time anyway for people to live through. My adolescence completely disappeared behind a wall of lack of confidence and certainty of failure. You put up a brave front and say words like independence and employment, but you just don't believe it.

Then, I found other blind people. It was quite by accident, and I am still grateful for that turn of fate. I encountered a blind person walking normally, setting his own course, deciding where he was going, and knowing where he was. We didn't speak. I just observed as he passed by. And, from that observation, I was sure that he knew where he was, not only in the building we were in, but in his life as well. I wanted to be able to do that.

I found out where he had learned to move about so confidently. There was a training program, run by blind people with blind people as teachers. But, that wasn't all. They were self-confident, successful, good at getting around. They knew where they were, and they were willing to teach me the skills. I was initially hesitant. Then I jumped in with both feet.

My sister has recently told me a story from that era. I don't remember this at all; it is a very clear childhood memory of hers. She is my baby sister, the one born eight years after me for whom I was the attentive big sister. When I lost my sight, it didn't matter to her. I was still her big sister, the one who had always taken care of her.

My sister and my mom came to visit me, she says, when I had been at the training program only a few weeks. While Mom talked with the teachers, I grandly announced that Martha and I were going for a walk. We come from a town of 8,000, and the program was in a town of 250,000. Lots of noise, lots of traffic, lots of ways to get hurt if you don't know what you are doing or where you are. My sister says that she remembers very clearly that my mom didn't hesitate. If I said I could take Martha for a walk, then Mom believed that I could. Martha, of course, never questioned whether I could. I was the big sister who had always taken care of her.

As I say, I remember none of this. Martha says now that the idea of our going for a walk must have been more than a simple matter to Mom. Here was her blind daughter, barely into the training program, planning to take the eight-year-old baby of the family out into the streets of a big city. But, Martha says that Mom didn't hesitate. We left.

I promptly got lost. Martha says that, as we walked (always safely on the sidewalk and crossing with the lights, of course), it slowly dawned on her that I didn't know where we were. But, she says that this didn't bother her since she knew her big sister would figure out what needed to be done. Martha says that I started asking her what she saw and when I got vague answers, would insist on her being precise about the location and angle from us that the objects were. As I got some more information, I figured out where we were and how to return to Mom. Martha says that, looking back, she does not remember any sense of worry or panic. She knew I would take care of her.

As I practiced under the guidance of fellow blind people to learn new ways of gathering information and using it to travel about safely and efficiently, the incidents of my not knowing where I was grew fewer and fewer. This was because my skill and my confidence were both being increased under practice and with the guidance of experienced blind persons. I was learning to know where I was.

The other thing that happened was that, when I did lose track of where I was, I learned how to find my way again. Using information as I was being taught by other blind people, I was learning what my little sister already knew—that I could find my way even when I had temporarily lost it. In fact, the final test in my training was for the teacher to get me deliberately disoriented and then to drop me off several miles from the training center. Using my own common sense and my developing skills, I had to find my way back. I did. That was the final proof to me that, even when I didn't know where I was, I could find out.

My family believed in me and encouraged me. But, they didn't know the skills and they couldn't be role models and they could always be dismissed by me as "not really understanding." But, other blind people, doing what I thought I couldn't, had taught me by their example, by their explicit instruction, by their generosity, that I could know where I am, both geographically and in the shaping of my own life. The lesson of learning to travel safely and efficiently, while it was vital in itself, spilled over to the rest of my view of myself. I found that self-confidence in myself that I had once so envied in that other self-confident blind person as he walked by.

My blind teachers, my blind friends, my blind colleagues all learned their self-confidence through the National Federation of the Blind, and I have learned also that the Federation is vital to my life. Not only did the Federation through its thousands of members around the country teach me how to believe in myself. The Federation also taught me something more.

It doesn't have to be like it was for me. If blind children can be reached, if their parents can be reached, if persons who lose their sight can be reached at an early point with the same message and the same examples and the same opportunities to learn where they are, then these blind men and women, boys and girls can learn right away what it took me so very long to learn: that, as a blind person, you can know where you are and you can know where you are going and you can make those decisions for yourself.

That is my hope for the Federation, that we can reach the blind people and all the sighted citizens as well with our message. My little sister had it right all along. It took me a little longer to get there. The judge hasn't quite figured it out yet. But, if we in the Federation keep spreading the message, he will.

Where am I? In the National Federation of the Blind and grateful to be there, grateful for the chance I received from Federation members and grateful for the chance to pass it on to others.

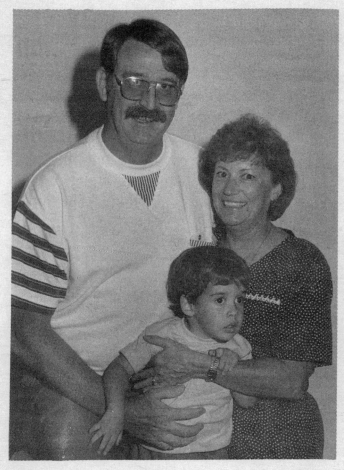

Ann and Dale Elliott with their son Caleb

THE TURNING POINT

Barbara Cheadle is the mother of a blind teen-ager and is president of the Parents of Blind Children Division of the National Federation of the Blind. She also edits Future Reflections, *our magazine for parents of blind children. Through Barbara I want you to meet Ann and Dale Elliott—also the parents of a blind child. Here is what Barbara Cheadle wrote recently in* Future Reflections:

I met Ann and Dale Elliott at the 1991 convention of the National Federation of the Blind. It was clear that they had come determined to learn all they could about blindness. They sought out parents, teachers, and blind adults of all ages. Everyone who met them must have been impressed, as was I, with their down-to-earth attitude and desire to learn. They also demonstrated courage. It isn't easy for parents to talk about a child's blindness when emotions are still raw and close to the surface. But with knowledge comes understanding, and with understanding comes healing. I was once asked by a parent when would her tears ever stop. I said something like this: "You are a parent; the tears never stop. However, the nature of your tears can change." That turning point comes much more surely if, like the Elliotts, you seek knowledge and understanding from those who know blindness best—the blind themselves. Here is Ann and Dale Elliott's story as told in their local newspaper, the *Times/Record News* of Wichita Falls, Texas, on Sunday, February 2, 1992:

"Big Brown Eyes":
Child's Blindness Helps Parents See
by Lois Luecke (Senior Staff Writer)

Ann and Dale Elliott still become teary-eyed when they talk about their adopted son, Caleb. Their tears are joyful, where once they were the tears of parents facing an unknown. Not until he was five months old did the Elliotts, older parents in their forties, discover that Caleb was blind.

"We were devastated," said Mrs. Elliott. "He has the prettiest big brown eyes. To look at him, you would never know that there's anything wrong." A number of people, Mrs. Elliott said, asked if they still wanted to keep Caleb. "Of course we did," she said. "He was ours."

The Elliotts' initial reaction, though, was one of disbelief and denial. They said they experienced various stages of grief, including anger and depression. Eye specialists told them that Caleb was born with a fatty buildup and a "pseudo cherry spot" on his retina. No name was given to it, and no one knows why, said his mother.

During that critical time, Mrs. Elliott says in retrospect, "I think probably I held my baby closer. My husband and I both cried, and we still do at times.... Then for the most part you accept it and go on with your life. But I don't think you ever get over the hurt. I don't think you feel so much for yourself, but for your child. And he doesn't need it. He doesn't know. His world is normal."

The Elliotts have come a long way in the three ensuing years. They believe they reached a major turning point only last July at the annual convention of the National Federation of the Blind in New Orleans.

Members of the NFB Parents Division, they heard talks by many of the nation's blind leaders. They saw sightless teen-agers making their way effortlessly through the convention halls, having fun. Role models like these and the Federation itself, they said, opened up new vistas for them and their son. "We have no doubt that Caleb will be a totally self-sufficient adult. We expect him to grow up and marry and have children. The only problem he has is that he can't see. But there is nothing to keep him from being a very successful adult. We intend to see he gets the best education he can get," said his mother.

Both parents are involved in all of Caleb's activities. They are learning Braille and encouraging Caleb to learn Braille by reading such books as a Sesame Street book on the A-B-C's. "His vision teacher Brailled sticky paper with every letter on each page. Another book is called a Twin Vision book. While you read the nursery rhymes to him, he feels the Braille. He doesn't know what it says, but this is getting his fingers accustomed to the feel of Braille."

The Elliotts are charter members of the NFB support group for parents with visually impaired children.

"Caleb is a typical 3-year-old. He is typical in every way except that he can't see. To him that's not a problem," said his mother, a licensed vocational nurse, who works for a physician at the Wichita Falls Clinic. Being blind from birth, Caleb can go anywhere in the house," said his father, a system operator with TU Electric. "He can tell you about anything in the house." Caleb still has light perception, and that helps him with balance and mobility. Sometimes he trails the wall with his hand when he goes down the hall, said his mother. They have taught him to keep his hands out so he won't bump into things. He uses a small cane when he goes outside and when the family goes to the mall or to a restaurant. In the near future his parents hope to buy a computer for him, with both Braille and regular printers.

Caleb and his parents enjoy unusual rapport. As they sat together for photographs in Caleb's room, they chatted and laughed, and Caleb kept up a running commentary about his "new toy," a balloon toy that "replaced an 'ailing' Kermit." The youngster runs over to the toy box in his room and pulls out a toy. As he does with most objects, he feels for the toy, puts it to his nose to smell, then to his mouth, and then to his ear to check the sound.

Dale and Ann Elliott said they have learned a great deal from Caleb and his acute senses of touch, sound, and smell.

"When we turn into our driveway, he says, 'We're home.' It's a 'soft ride,' because our driveway is smooth," in contrast to some of the rural roads around their house, Mrs. Elliott explained. "He can't see the mountains or the sky, everything that is beautiful," said Dale Elliott. "...But we went to Ruidoso on vacation last October. He just loved the mountains, the babbling brooks, the smell of the pine cones, the smell of the pine trees, and the feel of it all. He can probably tell you more about the mountains now than most people who go there."

Elliott's eyes brimmed with tears. "The first year he was blind, I would pray every night that the Lord would restore his vision. And now I pray every night, 'Thank you, God, for giving me such a fine boy.'"

Theodore Lubitz

THE BIOGRAPHY OF THEODORE PAUL LUBITZ

by Theodore Lubitz

A short time ago, Ted Lubitz, who is eighty-three, wrote to me and enclosed a copy of his life story. He thought that I might be interested in hearing what it was like to be blind in America during the early years of his long life. I was, and I believe the readers of the Kernel Book Series will be, too. His story has a simple eloquence and is a strong reminder of the vigor and toughness of those who have gone before and paved the road for us who have come after. Here it is:

I was born on August 21, 1909, at Marion, South Dakota. When I was real little, I lost my father and lived with my mother and my grandparents. My grandfather was a blacksmith, and my grandmother was a seamstress. My mother operated a cream station for the Bridgeman Russel Company of Sioux Falls.

When I was about four years old, I developed real sore eyes and had a lot of pain. My folks called a local doctor at Marion. He put the wrong medicine in my eyes, and it burned the corneas and the pupils, which gave me even more pain in my eyes. This left scars on both eyes when it healed. I could only see around the scars.

I was then taken to several doctors to see what they could do, but they could not do much for me. In the meantime I went to the Lutheran School at Marion. In the morning I learned German, and in the afternoon I learned English. School was hard for me because most of the work was done on the blackboard.

Later on we heard of a doctor at Omaha, Nebraska, and I was taken there. We stayed for a whole week, and at the last meeting the doctor said that the best thing for me was to attend the school for the blind.

That September I enrolled in the school for the blind at Gary, South Dakota, in 1921. I was already eleven years old. We could not really tell them what grade I was in, so I started all over in the first grade. It was hard for me to get used to reading Braille by touch, so I used my eyes. They had to put a blindfold on me. They found out that I had musical talent, so they put me on the violin and piano right away, along with my regular school work. I took violin, piano, making baskets, rug weaving, putting seats on chairs, making brooms, and so on.

In 1925 I was chosen to try to make my own violin. We had an employee who was a very fine violin maker. I worked every day after school and all day Saturdays on this violin, and in April I finished it.

I advanced very fast in my music. I did not like the piano as well as the violin. In 1928 I entered the high school music contest and won first place. When I got into high school, I started learning to become a piano tuner.

There was a girl at school named Agnes Redepenning who sort of fell for me, and that was fine with me. We sang a lot of duets together and attended all the school dances. I said to some of the students that "This is going to be my wife someday," and they all laughed! Agnes Redepenning started school the same year I did. We did not graduate together because Agnes was sick for a year and was taken out of school to live with her parents.

I practiced four hours a day on the violin. I was taking harmony, history of music, composition, and voice. I graduated in the spring of 1931, which was a bad time for anyone to finish school because of the Depression.

From 1921 until then there was very little done for the blind. There wasn't any employment for us. I had lost my grandmother in 1929, so I came home and put myself behind my stepfather and mother's table. The little money I made in piano tuning was just spending money once a week.

In 1938 I was contacted by the Williams Piano Company to work for them in Sioux Falls, so I went. It was better than staying at home. I lived in the YMCA. During that time I went to visit my girlfriend whenever I had a chance. Agnes and I prayed a lot about our marriage. We did not want to go into it unless it was right.

On March 23, 1941, Agnes and I married at Bellingham, Minnesota. The next day we went to Sioux Falls. In 1943 we moved to Watertown. I was called to Watertown by Al Williams, who was selling pianos and operating a second-hand store. Watertown at that time did not have a piano tuner. I have been here ever since. I have worked for Al Williams, David Piano Company, Art McCain's Music Store, and Alvin John's Music Store. I had my private work besides. When the Music Tree Store came to Watertown, I worked for them also. I had a driver for when I went out of town.

My wife was a very good cook, and her specialty was chicken and dumpling soup. She had a radio program every Sunday from Grace Lutheran Church for twenty-one years until she had to quit because of her health in 1971.

From that time on my wife's health went down hill, and she had to quit singing. You see, Agnes was a professional singer. She suffered a few little strokes, and each time it hampered her physically.

In December, 1987, Agnes suffered a very severe stroke, and in April she died. That was a great shock to me. I also landed in the hospital.

By the grace of God I have overcome all of my difficulties. Through prayer I have made it through my hardships. If it were not for the Lord, I could not function. God has been good to me. I am very happy. I have many friends!

I have several hobbies that I will tell you about. First, I am a Stephen Minister of the

Grace Lutheran Church. I have been in this for two years. I belong to a voice-spondence club all over the United States. I talk to people all over. Then I have my model trains, which I like to show people. I also have a reading class, where I have a book on tape and invite the folks to come and listen to the stories. Also I have the *Messiah* on recording at Christmas time.

I keep books on all my expenses and have done this for sixty-one years. I have a system where I set aside three percent of every item that I buy for an emergency fund and also the income. It works. I draw from this fund when I need some extra money. I do a lot of reading. I teach Braille to the elderly. I am teaching Braille to a lady who is losing her sight. I listen to a lot of classical music and tape some of it. I have a small library of cassette tapes.

Well, this is the story of my life, and I hope those of you who read it will find a blessing in it.

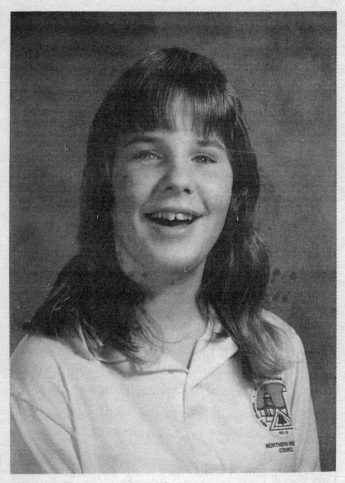

Rebecca Hart

THE TOURNAMENT OF ROSES

by Rebecca Hart

A twelve year-old girl marches in the Tournament of Roses. Not so unusual unless that twelve year-old is Rebecca Hart and is totally blind. On second thought, not so unusual even then—thanks to the National Federation of the Blind. We <u>are</u> changing what it means to be blind.

I just finished the most tiring, but exciting, two weeks of my life. I am in a Colonial Fife and Drum Corps called the Patriots. Mr. and Mrs. Evans, the band leaders, have been trying to get into the Tournament of Roses Parade for 17 years and finally they made it. I joined in January. I got asked to go on April 22.

This is an average parade year. It begins with the St. Patrick's Day Parade in March; the Apple Blossom and the Memorial Day Parades in May; the Fourth of July Parade;

an overnight trip and parade during the summer; the Labor Day Parade in September; the Halloween Parade in October; the Brunswick Parade in November; and the Christmas Parade in December. We have three practices a year which are about an hour and a half to three hours long. We also have our weekly music or drum lessons.

Getting ready for the Tournament of Roses was different. To begin with, the Rose Bowl crew had to stay at practice two hours after everyone else had gone. We had practices every Sunday in July, plus a few more after school started. It was OK, though, because everybody got to meet everybody else who was going. I should probably say here that there are 500 members in the Patriots, but only 175 went to California with 30 chaperons. When I was asked to go to the Tournament of Roses Parade it did not hit me until later what I was going to do. What I mean is that I did not know that the Tournament of Roses Parade was the biggest parade in the world.

When I march I carry Big Flag with seven other girls. It is also called the Colonial Colors. There are four poles on the flag and it takes two girls to carry each pole. The poles are threaded through the flag, and we carry the flag like it is lying down. When I first started in the Patriots I was on a banner with one or two other people. Then after my first year I asked Mrs. Evans if I could be on Big Flag, and she said yes.

During the first couple practices, when it was time for a break, my hands were shaking because I had been carrying the flag so long. In August the Big Flag girls had to go to practices with the fifers where we practiced marching. In November we had to march five and a half miles to prove that we could do it (the Tournament of Roses Parade route is five and one half miles long). We only had to do this once. On December 16 we had our last practice before leaving for California.

The parade started at about 8 a.m. California time. We were unit 78. Before we started marching we each got some candy from the Evans' to get our blood sugar high. As I said before, the parade route was five and a half miles long, but it did not seem like it because people were saying "Hi" and "Happy New Year" and things like that. I was kind of nervous when we were in front of the cameras, but I did fine. Some time later along the parade route someone yelled "Hi Becky Hart," but I do not know who it was.

I think the hardest part of the parade was marking time. That is when you march in place, and it is tiring because you build up this kind of rhythm and it is almost painful to stop. Once when we were marking time a parade official sprayed me in the face with water. He thought I looked "out of it." He did not know I was blind. When he found out he felt bad. But I was not startled; it felt good. I was the only one who was cool after that.

After the parade I went swimming. The motel had a pool and a hot tub, and while

I was in the hot tub I talked to some girls. We wished we could miss the train on Thursday. That night we went to Medieval Times. We pretended it was 1093. We ate dinner with our hands because silverware was not invented yet. Then we watched the knights perform.

It was a wonderful trip. I hope I will get to do this some time again soon.

Dianna Marie Maurer enjoys
an afternoon story read by Dad.

KEEPING WITHIN
THE LINES

by Marc Maurer

As readers of previous Kernel Books know, Marc Maurer is President of the National Federation of the Blind. He is a graduate of Notre Dame and the University of Indiana Law School and a member of the bar of several states and the United States Supreme Court. He is also the father of two young children. Braille is an important tool for him—in his career and in his home. Here is what he has to say about some of his early experiences with Braille:

The kindergarten in the public school that I attended when I was five left me with a feeling of alienation and frustration—though I didn't know the words to describe the problem. My teacher was a kind and gentle lady, who tried to help me, but I presented difficulties which she felt unable to solve. Many of the kindergarten activities were done visually. Learning colors, drawing, recognizing letters and numbers, naming the geometric shapes—all of these were presented visually. Some kindergarten tasks could be done quite effectively without sight—counting, reciting the alphabet, remembering your own address and telephone number, listing in order the days of the week or the months of the year. But in the drawing classes, I was unable to "keep within the lines," and "keeping within the lines" was important.

I learned the shapes of the print capital letters from the building blocks we had, and I came to know the forms of numbers in the same way. By the time kindergarten had come to an end, I had learned to print my name, MARC, but I usually got it backwards—CRAM. As I viewed it, the experiment with kindergarten was only marginally successful. Although it was never stated, the lesson of kindergarten was unmistakable— blind people are different from others; they require kindness; they can't do the ordinary things that other people do; they can't keep within the lines.

My parents decided that I would attend the school for the blind even though I would be away from home during most of the school year. Of course, I could return home for holidays and during some weekends, but the rest of the time I would live in a dormitory with my classmates at the school. At the age of six I left home. The school for the blind was over a hundred miles from our house. It was the beginning of a different kind of life.

Because I was at that time almost totally blind, I was expected to learn Braille. We started the learning process with flash cards. There was a straight line of Braille dots across the top of each card, and a single word in the center. I still remember the first flash card I ever read; it contained the word "go."

Each of us was given our first reading book—the primer about Dick and Jane and Spot. It was the first of the Braille books I have had in my hands. My book seemed to be about a foot square and about a half an inch thick. The teacher told us to open our books to page one.

My desk was in the first row, about the sixth or seventh from the front. The first child in the row was asked to read page one. When there were mistakes, the teacher corrected them.

Then, the second student was asked to read the same page. Again, when there were mistakes, the teacher corrected them. The lesson continued in the same manner. Each student in the first row was asked to read page one. By the time the teacher got to me, my job was clear, and my performance flawless. With my fingers on the page, I spoke the words of page one with never an error or hesitation. The teacher praised me highly and asked me to come to the front of the room. She produced a gold star from her desk drawer and pasted it to page one of my book. She told me to take my book home and show it to my mother. This is exactly what I did. On Friday night after the journey home, I proudly produced my primer, opened it to page one, and recited the words which appeared on the page.

My mother is a properly suspicious woman. She had learned Braille in the years before I attended school because she thought it might be helpful to me. She asked me if she could borrow the book, and of course I gave it to her. Later during the weekend she brought me a page of Braille and asked me to read it. Without much concern I confessed that I could not. My mother told me that it was an exact copy of page one of my book. I had memorized the words, but I was not able to read them.

During the summer between my first and second grade years, my mother took matters in hand. She told me that I must learn to read, and she said that she would teach me. For an hour every morning I was going to study Braille. I complained. The other kids got to go outside to play, but I could not. Nobody else had summer school at home—

only me. But none of my griping did any good. My mother had made up her mind; I was going to learn to read.

When I returned to the school for the blind for my second grade year, I discovered the library of Braille books—that collection of sweet-smelling Braille volumes almost a foot square and about two and a half inches thick. During the next four years I read every book that the librarian would let me have. I developed the habit of reading at night. Blindness has some advantages. I would slide the book under the bed sometime during the evening. Bedtime was 8:00. The house parent made his rounds between 8:30 and 8:45. I could hear his shoes coming down the hall and then receding in the distance. When the footsteps had faded, the book came out. No light is needed for Braille. Sometimes it was cold, but the Braille book would fit under the covers.

I tried the same system at home, and it worked most of the time. When I got caught, which happened occasionally, my mother spanked me. The punishments were fair, but the reading was worth it.

Although I complained bitterly about learning Braille, I am most grateful to my mother for insisting that I learn it. How fortunate I am that she understood the necessity for me to read. How fortunate I am that she was persistent and demanding. How fortunate I am that she had learned Braille herself and was able to teach me.

Today, we in the National Federation of the Blind do much to help make Braille available to blind students and to encourage the teaching of Braille both to children and adults who are blind. But this is not how it has always been. There was a time when Braille was regarded as inferior, and all too often today it does not get the attention it deserves. Much of my work as a lawyer could not have been done without Braille. I now read to my children most evenings. They enjoy the stories, and I enjoy the reading as much as they do. How different my life would have been without the ability to read Braille. How different it can be for the children of this generation if we give them the chance to learn. The message should not be that blind people are different and unable to take part. Even though I might not be able to draw, my mother felt certain that I could keep within the lines. We in the National Federation of the Blind are doing what we can to make it come true.

President Maurer speaks
at the annual convention of the
National Federation of the Blind.

National Federation of the Blind

You can help us spread the word...

...about our Braille Readers Are Leaders contest for blind schoolchildren, a project which encourages blind children to achieve literacy through Braille.

...about our scholarships for deserving blind college students.

...about Job Opportunities for the Blind, a program that matches capable blind people with employers who need their skills.

...about where to turn for accurate information about blindness and the abilities of the blind.

Most importantly, you can help us by sharing what you've learned about blindness in these pages with your family and friends. If you know anyone who needs assistance with the problems of blindness, please write:

Marc Maurer, President
1800 Johnson Street, Suite 300
Baltimore, Maryland 21230-4998
Your contribution is tax-deductible.